LIGHT FROM CYPRUS ON THE GREEK 'DARK AGE'?

THE NINETEENTH
J. L. MYRES MEMORIAL LECTURE

LIGHT FROM CYPRUS
ON THE
GREEK 'DARK AGE'?

A Lecture delivered at

The Ashmolean Museum, Oxford, on 5th May, 1997

by

J. N. COLDSTREAM

LEOPARD'S HEAD PRESS

1998

Published in 1998 by
LEOPARD'S HEAD PRESS LIMITED
1–5 Broad Street, Oxford OX1 3AW

ISBN 0 904920 37 2

Typeset by Denham House, Yapton, West Sussex
and printed in Great Britain by
Blackmore Press, Longmead, Shaftesbury, Dorset

LIGHT FROM CYPRUS ON THE GREEK 'DARK AGE'?

LADIES AND GENTLEMEN,

Sir John Myres is justly revered today as the true father of Cypriot Archaeology, *per se* and *qua* Cypriot. His predecessor, Max Ohnefalsch-Richter, had assembled an impressive corpus of Cypriot antiquities in his *magnum opus*, but chiefly as a background to Homer and the Bible.[1] Others, both his contemporaries and his successors, saw Cyprus either as an eastern extension of the Classical Greek world[2] or, in prehistoric times, as a 'peripheral area' at the outer edge of the older civilizations in the Ancient Near East.[3] But Myres, through his long experience as a field archaeologist and as a specialist in the archaeology of Cyprus,[4] came to be the first scholar to appreciate the individual flavour of the island's antiquity. In this respect, a good example of his contribution is his treatment of Cypriot Archaic sculpture,[5] in which he demonstrated that the first life-size figures could not possibly have anything to do with Greece. If from anywhere, in his view, they owed something — probably at several removes — to Assyria; but already they displayed a forceful and vigorous local Cypriot style, to be further defined by Gjerstad[6] through the copious discoveries of the Swedish Cyprus Expedition.

These early sculptures, however, belong to the very end of my story, which goes back to the beginning of the Early Iron Age. In Greece, in spite of recent discoveries, this is still an age that can be called 'dark'; an age of total illiteracy and, in most Aegean regions, an age of poverty, poor communications, and isolation from the outside world. Meanwhile Cyprus, through its closer proximity to the founts of civilization in the Near East, experienced an age no darker than subfusc. In what ways, then — on the assumption of *ex oriente lux* — could Cyprus have helped to lighten this Greek 'Dark Age'? On this question, new thoughts have been

1 M. Ohnefalsch-Richter, *Kypros, the Bible and Homer*, Berlin and London,1893. Richter did, however, join Myres in producing the first *Catalogue of the Cyprus Museum*, Nicosia, 1899.

2 E.g. A. W. Lawrence, *Journal of Hellenic Studies*, 46, 1926, 163–70; F. N. Pryce, *Catalogue of Sculpture, Department of Greek and Roman Antiquities in the British Museum*, I.2; *Cypriote and Etruscan*, 1931, 3–11; S. Casson, *Ancient Cyprus*, London, 1937, 169–92.

3 E.g. G. Perrot and C. Chipiez, *Histoire de l'Art dans l'Antiquité*, III, Paris, 1885, 490–506 (I owe this reference to Dr R. S. Merrillees); H. Frankfort, *The Art and Architecture of the Ancient Orient*, 4th edn., Harmondsworth, 1970, 322; 'Cyprus, in any case, may be reckoned as part of the Phoenician cultural orbit.'

4 Summarized by V. Karageorghis, *The Archaeology of Cyprus: the Ninety Years after Myres*, 13th J. L. Myres Memorial Lecture, Oxford, 1987, 3–5; A. H. S. Megaw, *Report of the Department of Antiquities, Cyprus*, 1988.2, 282–3.

5 J. L. Myres, *Handbook of the Cesnola Collection of Antiquities from Cyprus*, New York, 1914, 123–39; *idem., Annual of the British School at Athens*, 41 (1940–45), 100–4, answering Hellenocentric views mentioned in n.2.

6 E. Gjerstad, *The Swedish Cyprus Expedition*, vol. IV.2, Lund, 1948, 94–103.

stimulated by many new discoveries. First, we know that Greek Protogeometric pottery, apparently of Euboean type, was already reaching the Phoenician metropolis of Tyre, probably via Cyprus, from well back in the tenth century B.C.[7] In the Aegean, we have a great variety of orientalia from the rich graves of Lefkandi in Euboea,[8] and from the family tombs in the North Cemetery of Knossos in Crete.[9] In Cyprus, other new cemetery excavations provoke more new thoughts. In Old Paphos, at the site of Kouklia *Skales*,[10] the earliest and richest tombs of the eleventh and tenth centuries allow us our first glimpse of Greek literacy in Cyprus, besides lending ample confirmation to Gjerstad's description of the Cypro-Geometric I phase as a dynamic and creative period in the island's history.[11] And at Amathus, stronghold of the indigenous Eteocypriots, the huge abundance of finds from newly excavated tombs[12] include a steady flow of pottery from Greece — exports that closely match those reaching Tyre,[13] and therefore place Amathus firmly on the route from the Aegean to the Phoenician metropolis.

Here, though, one need not elaborate on the intermediary role of Cyprus in relaying oriental notions to the Aegean, since the theme of 'Cyprus between the Orient and the Occident' has already been explored in numerous articles and international gatherings.[14] Instead, the questions that I would like to consider are: what skills, what civilized amenities and what artistic ideas did Cyprus in particular contribute towards the alleviation of the Greek 'Dark Age'? My discussion will range widely in time between the eleventh and seventh centuries B.C., and this long period can be divided into two approximately equal halves, before and after the foundation of the Tyrian colony of Kition.

The eleventh century is the age of the main migrations of Aegean peoples to Cyprus, during a time of commotion on the island when Enkomi, and other major centres of the Late Bronze Age, were finally deserted. The new immigrants chose to make a fresh start by settling in new coastal sites that were to grow into the capitals of the historical Greek Cypriot kingdoms: Salamis, Lapithos, Soli, Marion, Old Paphos, Kourion, among others. We have become accustomed to thinking of

---

7 J. N. Coldstream and P. M. Bikai, *Report of the Department of Antiquities, Cyprus*, 1988.2, 35–44.

8 *Lefkandi*, I (1980); II.1, (1990); II.2, (1993); III, plates, (1996). For the most recent general survey, M. R. Popham, in *The Archaeology of Greek Colonisation*, eds. G. R. Tsetskhladze and F. De Angelis, Oxford, 1994., 11–34.

9 *Knossos, the North Cemetery: Early Greek Tombs*, eds., J. N. Coldstream and H. W. Catling, *Annual of the British School at Athens*, Suppl. 28, 1996, 721.

10 V. Karageorghis, *Alt-Paphos*, III; *Palaepaphos-Skales, an Iron Age Cemetery in Cyprus*, Mainz, 1983.

11 E. Gjerstad, *The Swedish Cyprus Expedition*, vol. IV.2, Lund, 1948, 435.

12 *Études Chypriotes*, VIII; *la Nécropole d'Amathonte, Tombes 113–367*, 6 vols., eds.,V. Karageorghis, O. Picard and C. Tytgat, Nicosia, 1987–92; C. Tytgat and J. N. Coldstream, *Report of the Department of Antiquities, Cyprus*, 1995, 137–98 (Tomb NW 194); J. N. Coldstream, *Report of the Department of Antiquities, Cyprus*, 1995, 199–214 (Greek imports from tombs most recently excavated by the Department of Antiquities.)

13 *Art. cit.*, (n.7), 42, fig. 1.

14 E.g. J. Pouilloux, *Chypre entre l'Orient et Occident*, Bank of Cyprus, Nicosia, 1985; *Cyprus between the Orient and the Occident*, ed. V. Karageorghis, Nicosia, 1986; J. N. Coldstream, 'Early Greek visitors to Cyprus and the Eastern Mediterranean', in *Cyprus and the East Mediterranean in the Iron Age*, ed. V. Tatton-Brown, British Museum, 1989, 90–6.

these newcomers as unfortunate refugees escaping from the final collapse of Aegean Bronze Age civilization, at least a century after the demise of the Mycenaean palaces. But we could also see them as optimists[15] and opportunists, already well informed from earlier Mycenaean visitors about the island's rich copper resources; and, because of a much closer access to Near Eastern amenities, they could look forward to a more peaceful life than would have been possible in a devastated and beleaguered Aegean world already entering a deep recession. One might wonder whether their arrival was wholly welcome to the indigenous people of Cyprus. At all events, they arrived in whole communities, and in sufficient force to establish themselves in their new coastal sites. We know virtually nothing of their settlements, but in their new cemeteries — Kourion *Kaloriziki*, Palaepaphos *Skales* and Lapithos *Kastros*, for example — many well-furnished tombs are outstandingly rich in comparison with the modest contents of indigenous cemeteries, giving us the impression that the Aegean immigrants soon established an aristocracy of wealth on the island.[16]

During this age of migration there must have been much coming and going between Cyprus and the Aegean;[17] and it is not surprising that, in these turbulent times, it is the warriors, the soldiers of fortune, who have left the clearest archaeological record as travellers. Travels usually involve some exchange of ideas; and, in view of the much happier state of affairs in Cyprus than in the Aegean, one would expect any really useful ideas to have come from East to West, rather that vice versa. So it is with the warriors who are among the first incumbents — and perhaps the founders — of the North Cemetery at Knossos, cremated in pit graves. This kind of tomb, a rare alternative to the usual rock-cut chamber with long dromos, nevertheless has Minoan antecedents:[18] a deep rectangular pit opening at the base into one or more miniature caves. Tomb 186, with a single cave, housed a single warrior; the triple complex of Tomb 201 produced the cremated remains of a woman, possibly a child, and another warrior.[19] Hector Catling has placed the warriors in a Homeric setting, as 'heroes returned'; returned from wanderings that had clearly included Cyprus, to judge from a strong Cypriot element in the offerings, unusually rich for their time.[20] With the lady went a necklace of 80 gold beads, and a pair of gold rosettes for attachment to her dress, an ornament well

15 J. N. Coldstream, 'What sort of Migration?', in *Cyprus in the 11th Century B.C.*, ed. V. Karageorhis, Nicosia, 1994, 143–6.

16 J. N. Coldstream, 'Status symbols in Cyprus in the eleventh century B.C.', in *Early Society in Cyprus*, ed. E. Peltenburg, Edinburgh, 1989, 325–35.

17 V. R. d'A Desborough, *The Greek Dark Ages*, London, 1972, 340–2.

18 H. W. Catling, in *Knossos, the North Cemetery: Early Greek Tombs*, eds., J. N. Coldstream and H. W. Catling, *Annual of the British School at Athens*, Suppl. 28, 1996, 640, 642–3.

19 H. W. Catling, in *Knossos, the North Cemetery: Early Greek Tombs*, eds., J. N. Coldstream and H. W. Catling, *Annual of the British School at Athens*, Suppl. 28, 1996, 190–9, figs. 43, 123, 163–6; pls. 33c–c, 34, 183, 274–80.

20 H. W. Catling, 'Heroes returned? Subminoan burials from Crete', in *The Ages of Homer: a Tribute to E. T. Vermeule*, eds. J. B. Carter and S. P. Morris, Austin, Texas, 1995, 123–36.

matched in a roughly contemporary Cypriot tomb at Salamis; also a handsome and unusually ornate Subminoan stirrup-jar, influenced by the contemporary and much stronger Proto-White-Painted style of Cyprus,[21] itself largely of Aegean derivation. From the debris of the warrior's pyre came many charred scraps of bronze, including representations of birds, animals, and the wing perhaps of a sphinx. Among these fragments the expert eye of Dr Catling has identified one of those four-sided bronze stands with openwork figured decoration, made in Cyprus no later than the early twelfth century,[22] and so already a century old when deposited in this tomb. Here, then, is the first of a long series of valuable antiques from Cyprus, to be treasured in various Greek contexts throughout the Early Iron Age.

The two warriors had an impressive array of military gear. Quite apart from bronze swords and spearheads, there were bosses — most probably for shields — and the remains of a boar's tusk helmet, that notoriously transferable piece of Homeric equipment.[23] They also possessed two types of object which, in an eleventh-century context, are very likely to have come from Cyprus: the whetstones, and the large bronze projectiles, far heavier than the arrowheads of the Aegean.[24] But the most innovative articles are in *iron*, two blades belonging to the warrior of Tomb 186; a bimetallic knife of Cypriot type with bronze rivets on the handle, a type which had already been circulating in Greece for about two generations;[25] and a dirk, 26 cms. long which, together with another in a contemporary burial of a warrior in Tiryns — another travelling 'samurai' — is one of the very earliest offensive weapons in Greece to be made in the new metal.[26] Even if these are local products, the techniques for making them were most probably learned from smiths settled in Cyprus, in the wake of the great Aegean migrations; for iron technology had already been acquired in Cyprus by the late twelfth century,[27] and no language barrier would have stood between teacher and pupil in explaining the

21 H. W. Catling, in *Knossos, the North Cemetery: Early Greek Tombs*, eds., J. N. Coldstream and H. W. Catling, *Annual of the British School at Athens*, Suppl. 28, 1996, 301.

22 H. W. Catling, 'Workshop and Heirloom: Prehistoric Bronze Stands in the East Mediterranean', *Report of the Department of Antiquities, Cyprus*, 1984, 69–91. The fragments from Knossos Tomb 201 are illustrated there in pl. 15.1–3, 5–6.

23 *Iliad*, x.261–71; H. W. Catling, in *Knossos, the North Cemetery: Early Greek Tombs*, eds., J. N. Coldstream and H. W. Catling, *Annual of the British School at Athens*, Suppl. 28, 1996, 534–5, 647.

24 H. W. Catling, in *Knossos, the North Cemetery: Early Greek Tombs*, eds., J. N. Coldstream and H. W. Catling, *Annual of the British School at Athens*, Suppl. 28, 1996, 521–2.

25 E. Tholander, *OpAth*, 10, 1971, 15–22; V. R. d'A. Desborough, *op. cit.*, (n. 17), 315–16, 340–1; A. M. Snodgrass in *The Coming of the Age of Iron*, eds. T. A. Wertime and J. D. Muhly, New Haven and London, 1980, 335–74; S. Sherratt in *op. cit.*, (n. 15), 59–106, esp. 86–7 giving a list of 44 twelfth-century iron tools and weapons from Cyprus.

26 H. W. Catling, in *Knossos, the North Cemetery: Early Greek Tombs*, eds., J. N. Coldstream and H. W. Catling, *Annual of the British School at Athens*, Suppl. 28, 1996, 528–9; Tiryns: N. Verdelis, *AM*, 78, 1963, 14–16, Beil, 5.4 (bottom) and fig. 5.

27 A. M. Snodgrass, 'Cyprus and the Beginnings of Iron Technology in the Eastern Mediterranean', in *Early Metallurgy in Cyprus*, eds. J. D. Muhly, R. Maddin and V. Karageorghis, Nicosia, 1982, 285–95.

difficult process of carburization, with its very sensitive control of temperature in repeated heating and cooling.[28]

This Cretan warrior clearly rejoiced in the cutting edge of the new metal, superior to that of the bronze weapons wielded by his Minoan or Mycenaean forebears. Quite soon, however, iron was put to use for dress ornaments, for which it proved to be not at all suitable; most notably, in the Protogeometric graves in the Kerameikos cemetery of Athens, for fibulae, long pins and other ornaments.[29] For much of that period, the Athenian graves contained no bronze. For this lack of bronze, two explanations have been proposed:[30] either an enthusiasm for novelty in exploring to the utmost what could be made in the new metal, or an acute shortage of bronze, caused by what once seemed to be a total isolation of the Aegean world from the sources of the bronze metals in Cyprus and the Near East,[31] so that iron was pressed into service as a poor substitute, to manufacture small objects that were better made in bronze. But now, somewhere in the middle of this supposed period of bronze stortage, we have the earliest exports of Greek Iron Age pottery to Tyre, of Euboean type.[32] These include skyphoi with full concentric circles, well matched in the abundant deposit of Middle Protogeometric pottery of the early tenth century, associated with the hugh apsidal building on the Toumba of Lefkandi.[33] No longer, then, can it be said that the Aegean was totally cut off from eastern metal sources at this time, for it is hard to believe that a Euboean ship returning from Tyre would not have called at Kition or Amathus to load up with Cypriot copper ore, if it had so wished. If indeed bronze was scarce in Protogeometric Greece — and here the negative evidence voices only a very faint 'no'[34] — then one must think instead of the alternative explaination, an over-enthusiastic conversion to iron in the Aegean. Indeed, it is quite natural for new ideas to be carried to excess, before their novelty wears off, and they eventually find their proper function, and their limitations. By the end of the tenth century, most pins and fibulae were once again made in the more elegant medium of bronze.

If the Greeks had learned their iron technology from Cyprus in the eleventh century, it might seem rather paradoxical that the Cypriots should also be helping them towards a reviving bronze industry in the late tenth century, most clearly documented in the settlement on the Xeropolis plateau of Lefkandi; but that is the import of Dr Catling's[35] study of the terracotta moulds found there in the earliest

28 On the process of carburization see A. M. Snodgrass, *The Dark Age of Greece*, Edinburgh, 1971, 214–17; T. Stech, J. D. Muhly and R. Maddin, *Report of the Department of Antiquities, Cyprus*, 1985, 192–3.

29 E.g. *Kerameikos*, I, pl. 76; *Kerameikos*, IV, pl. 39.

30 V. R. d'A Desborough, *The Greek Dark Ages*, London, 1972, 317–18.

31 A. M. Snodgrass, *The Dark Age of Greece*, Edinburgh, 1971, 237–9.

32 T. Stech, J. D. Muhly and R. Maddin, *Report of the Department of Antiquities, Cyprus*, 1988.2, 39, pl. 10, nos. 19, 25–7.

33 M. R. Popham *et al.*, *Antiquity*, 56, 1982, 171–2, fig. 4; cf. *Lefkandi*, II.1, pl. 48.120.

34 E.g. for Athens, A. M. Snodgrass, *The Dark Age of Greece*, Edinburgh, 1971, 233.

35 H. W. Catling in *Lefkandi*, I, 93–7, pls. 12, 13a.

known stratum of the Iron Age — moulds for bronze tripod legs, decorated with false spirals. We know this motif already on two classes of tripod leg whose manufacture is separated by four centuries; first, on the much earlier rod tripods made in Cyprus no later than the twelfth century, but appearing as antiques in much later Aegean contexts;[36] second, on the much later Greek tripod cauldrons offered at the Panhellenic sanctuaries of Olympia and Delphi, probably of the early eighth century, the oldest class of monumental vessels already enlarged for prestige far beyond what is useful in daily life.[37] The tripod legs cast in the Lefkandi moulds, about 5 cms. wide, would be intermediate in size, as well as in date, between those two classes; and so Dr Catling supposes the presence at Lefkandi of 'a bronze-smith trained in the East, working as an itinerant craftsman. What is more, he may well have brought with him the materials he needed for his work, as well as his expertise.' This craftsman would thus have forestalled the later monumental tripod cauldrons by placing the false spirals between parallel ridges. If we now bear in mind the wide circulation of the old Cypriot rod tripods as antiques, an interesting question arises: could the skill for making these tripod legs have been acquired solely through native invention, borrowing a decorative motif from an antique rod tripod stand? Or is the skill so sophisticated that it requires tuition from an immigrant eastern smith, as Dr Catling implies? He has good reason to be sceptical of the bronze shortage theory, on the grounds that a *newly revived* bronze industry at Lefkandi is not likely to have started up at such a high level of metallurgical skill. At present, we do not know of any earlier Iron Age habitation on the Xeropolis plateau before the late tenth century context of the moulds; but only a very small part of the settlement has been dug, and we have come to know from experience how hazardous it is to make any negative statement about Lefkandi. Meanwhile, recent finds from Cyprus cannot help us very far in resolving this question. The only relevant bronze there is the tripod cauldron from one of the richest tombs in the *Skales* cemetery of Old Paphos, no. 58; the context is Cypro-Geometric I, *c.*1050 to 950 B.C., and so at least 50 years older than the Lefkandi moulds. The type is wholly Greek, with Late Mycenaean antecedents — possibly brought over by one of the founders of the Greek settlement of Old Paphos. It corresponds to the very earliest class at Olympia with solid, massive legs, polygonal in section — a type which was to be superseded by the first monumental tripod cauldrons to which I have referred. Our smith of Lefkandi, whether or not his false spirals identify him as an immigrant Cypriot, did manage to forestall the technique of the monumental vessels by experimentally devising a broad and flat leg, for which the saving of bronze would be the first step towards enlargement to a monumental size. But if

36 H. W. Catling, *Cypriot Bronzework in the Mycenaean World*, Oxford, 1964, 190–223, pls. 27–32; on the dating, *idem.*, *Report of the Department of Antiquities, Cyprus*, 1984, 72.

37 B. Schweitzer, *Greek Geometric Art*, London, 1971, 180–1, Type II, e.g. pl. 217. On Schweitzer's unacceptably late dating of the Cypriot rod tripods (*op. cit.*, 164–7), see *Gnomon*, 44, 1972, 599–600. Their influence on the monumental tripod legs, *direct* according to Schweitzer, can now be more plausibly seen as *indirect* in the light of the Lefkandi moulds, discovered after the completion of Schweitzer's *magnum opus* in 1964.

his experiment is in any way ancestral to the great monumental tripod cauldrons of Olympia and Delphi, then the intervening stages have yet to be found.

So much, then, for the metallurgical contributions from Cyprus towards lightening of the Greek 'Dark Age'; the new expertise in working iron, at least, was a skill as yet unknown in the prosperous days of the Mycenaean palaces. We should now consider the effect of those large bronze antiques dating from the end of the Cypriot Bronze Age — antiques which, when circulating in much later contexts of the Aegean 'Dark Age', would have been objects of wonder. Their circulation, no doubt, was greatly assisted by those travelling warriors who, during an age of disruption, wandered between the Aegean and the Eastern Mediterranean, acquiring them either as booty or as guest gifts.[38] Because of their exotic rarity, they might often be handed down through several generations as precious heirlooms from a more glorious bygone age. One such relic is a large pair of bronze wheels fixed to their axle, from Grave 39 in the royal Toumba cemetery of Lefkandi in a late tenth-century context.[39] Most probably, the wheels supported a four-sided figure stand, like some of those made in Cyprus towards the end of the Bronze Age;[40] but, with a diameter of 25 cms., the wheels are larger than any known stand. They are exceeded in size only by similar stands described in the first *Book of Kings*,[41] given by Hiram of Tyre to furnish Solomon's new temple in Jerusalem: 10 'bases of brass' decorated with 'lions, oxen and cherubim', and resting on wheels one and half cubits high. Here nothing survives from the body of a figured stand, but, about two generations earlier, we have a figured antique from Cyprus, also in bronze, in the large amphoroid krater which became the king's cremation urn[42] in the spacious royal shaft grave inside the Toumba building. In spite of its fragmentary state, the whole rim is preserved, decorated in relief with a hunting scene in which men attack lions and bulls with bow and arrow. The context of this burial is Middle Protogeometric, in the first half of the tenth century; and it so happens that a more modest Lefkandi grave of just this time has produced, among its pottery, a small hydria[43] bearing two tiny and very schematic archers, by far the earliest experiment in figured vase-painting from Euboea in the Early Iron Age. This coincidence of theme — and, for Greece, an unusual one — shows how the visual imagination of local Greek craftsmen could be stimulated by a view of exotic antiques from Cyprus, however crude and simple their efforts might seem to us. Such pictures help to fill

---

38 H. W. Catling in *op. cit.*, (n. 15), 96–7.

39 M. R. Popham *et al.*, *Annual of the British School at Athens*, 77, 1982, 219, T. 39.30, fig. 8, pl. 34; H. W. Catling, *Report of the Department of Antiquities, Cyprus*, 1984, 82, pl. 11.5; *Lefkandi*, III, pls. 43, 147.

40 E.g. H. W. Catling, *op. cit.*, (n. 36), 207–10, pls. 35–6.

41 I *Kings*, vii, 27–37; H. W. Catling, *Report of the Department of Antiquities, Cyprus*, 1984, 86, n. 57.

42 M. R. Popham *et al.*, *Antiquity*, 56, 1982, 172–3, pl. 24, and in *Lefkandi*, II.2, 19–21, pl. 16; discussion by H. W. Catling, *ibid.*, 81–96.

43 *Lefkandi*, I, 127, S. 51.2, fig. 4, pls. 106, 210b–c. From spectrographic analysis the fabric appeared to be atypical, possibly imported, but 'probably made not far from Lefkandi', V. R. d'A. Desborough in *op. cit.*, 348, n. 477.

what J. L. Benson describes as the 'long, pictureless hiatus'[44] in Greek figured art — the absence of any assured tradition of representational drawing between the Mycenaean collapse and the renaissance of the eighth century. This apparent lack of figured art is one of the more poignant aspects of the alleged 'Dark Age' of Greece — an age which could not, so it seemed, communicate itself to us through contemporary pictures.

It is in Crete, however, where new discoveries have contributed most to filling in this 'pictureless hiatus'; indeed, almost every generation of the Cretan 'Dark Age' can now show at least one experimental figured vase, mainly among recent finds from the cemeteries of Knossos.[45] For some of these early experiments one suspects that the inspiration came not from the East, but from the rediscovery of Minoan antiques, of which the largest and most easily visible would have been the clay larnakes of the fourteenth and thirteenth centuries, with their pictorial decoration, sometimes put to re-use in tombs of the Dark Age;[46] for example, there is an obvious link between the splendid Goddess with birds and spiral trees on a late ninth-century cremation urn from Tomb 107 in the North Cemetery, and a similar scene on a fine but much battered Minoan larnax made five centuries earlier, and yet *found in the same tomb*.[47]

Here, though, we are more concerned with the impact of Eastern — and especially Cypriot — iconography; and impact seen at its most dramatic in the gruesome picture on the Lion krater from Teke Tomb E, of around 850 B.C.[48] A desperate warrior is in some danger of being consumed by two hungry lions — a theme without precedent in the art of the Aegean Bronze Age, for Mycenaean heroes are never allowed to be outnumbered by lions; but there is a similar portrayal in relief on a cast ring of a Cypriot four-sided bronze stand in the British Museum from Kourion;[49] and, as we have seen among the possessions of the Subminoan warrior in Tomb 201, we now know that such stands, like the related rod tripods from the same workshops, were also among the precious Cypriot antiques circulating in Crete during the Early Iron Age.[50]

44 J. L. Benson, *Horse, Bird and Man*, Amherst, 1970, 10.

45 J. N. Coldstream, 'Some Minoan Reflexions in Cretan Geometric Art', in *Studies in honour of T. B. L. Webster*, II, eds. J. H. Betts, J. T. Hooker and J. R. Green, Bristol, 1988, 23–32.

46 J. N. Coldstream, 'Some Nostalgic Knossians of the Ninth Century B.C.', *Prak. Akad. Athenōn*, 71B, 1996, 240–62.

47 J. N. Coldstream, 'A Protogeometric Nature Goddess from Knossos', *Bulletin of the Institute of Classical Studies (London)*, 31, 1984, 93–104, esp. 99–100; H. W. Catling, in *Knossos, the North Cemetery: Early Greek Tombs*, eds., J. N. Coldstream and H. W. Catling, *Annual of the British School at Athens*, Suppl. 28, 1996, 148–51, fig. 109, pls. 155–6. On the larnax, L. Morgan, *Annual of the British School at Athens*, 82, 1987, 171–200.

48 L. H. Sackett, *Annual of the British School at Athens*, 71, 1976, 117–29, pls. 15, 16; J. N. Coldstream, in *Knossos, the North Cemetery: Early Greek Tombs*, eds., J. N. Coldstream and H. W. Catling, *Annual of the British School at Athens*, Suppl. 28, 1996, 371.

49 H. W. Catling, *op. cit.*, (n. 36), pl. 35b.

50 Knowledge of the Cypriot four-sided stands is also implied by the clay copy from Karphi (*Annual of the British School at Athens*, 38, 1937–38, pl. 34) and by fragmentary eighth-century imitations in Crete; J. Boardman, *The Cretan Collection in Oxford*, Oxford, 1961, 132–3, Idaean Cave and Teke tholos; A. Lembesi, *Praktika Tès Archaiologikès Etaireias (Athens)*, 1972, 198; 1973, 190, pl. 188a; 1974, 227, pl. 168a; 1975, 329, pl. 259, all from Kato Symi.

The reverse side of the same krater presents us with another scene of eastern character: a pair of confronted sphinxes,[51] wearing conical helmets of oriental type, quite distinct from the flat polos caps worn by such creatures in the representations of the Aegean Bronze Age. For this scene the eastern source is likely to have been contemporary rather than antique; that is, the imagery in relief, inside the bronze bowls with figured decoration. At least a dozen of them have been recorded from Crete,[52] but without any closely datable contexts; but we now know that they were circulating in the Aegean as early as the tenth century, thanks to the closed contexts in the single graves of Lefkandi. In Grave 55 of the Toumba cemetery there,[53] with pottery of c. 900 B.C., a bronze bowl is decorated with antithetic pairs of heraldic sphinxes, massive in build, and not unlike those on the Teke krater except for the different treatment of the wings. The Knossian vase-painter has omitted the central member of the oriental composition, the Sacred Tree; but the sphinxes' gesture of raising their foremost paws, meaningless on the krater, is explained on the bronze bowl, where they reverently salute the Tree in time-honoured fashion, as in several representations from the Late Bronze Age of Cyprus.[54] Whether this bowl came from Cyprus or from North Syria we cannot at present tell; but one could argue a Cypriot origin for a still earlier import, the badly corroded bronze bowl from Grave 70 in the same cemetery.[55] Here, too, we have heraldic sphinxes again, saluting the Tree: the rest of the frieze shows a cult scene extra-ordinarily similar in style and iconography to that on the well-known bronze bowl in New York, which Cesnola claimed to have found in a tomb at Idalion.[56] In both scenes we have a seated goddess with musicians behind her, approached by a procession of women bearing offerings, the procession being interrupted by a horned altar and a table with vases on it. In addition, the 'rustic and uncouth' human faces, with bulging eyes, are so similar that this bowl from Lefkandi should be added to the earliest stage of the class which Gjerstad defined as Proto-Cypriot.[57] In his view, the Idalion bowl was its oldest example, which he dated around 800 B.C. — a date which, in view of the tenth-century context of the new Lefkandi bowl, may now need to be raised by at least a hundred years.

From new eastern images let us turn back briefly to newly recovered skills. At Lefkandi, at the time when this bowl arrived as an import, we have already seen

51 *Annual of the British School at Athens*, 71, 1976, 124, fig. 6.

52 G. Markoe, *Phoenician Bronze and Silver Bowls from Cyprus and the Mediterranean*, Berkeley, 1985, 162–9.

53 M. R. Popham in *The Archaeology of Greek Colonisation*, eds. G. R. Tsetskhladze and F. De Angelis, Oxford, 1994, 17–20, fig. 2.7; *AR*, 35, 1989, 118, 121, fig. 5; *Lefkandi*, III, pls. 63, 133, 144.

54 E.g. on Cypriot cylinder seals: E. Porada, *American Journal of Archaeology*, 52, 1948, 187–8, nos. 16–17, pl. 9; A. Dessenne, *Le sphinx: étude iconographique*, I, Paris, 1957, 80, nos. 196, 198, pls. 16, 33. I owe these references to Mrs C. D'Albiac who is preparing a study of Cypriot sphinxes and griffins.

55 M. R. Popham in *The Archaeology of Greek Colonisation*, eds. G. R. Tsetskhladze and F. De Angelis, Oxford, 1994, 17–19, fig. 2.8; *Lefkandi*, III, pls. 70, 134, 145.

56 For full bibliography see G. Markoe, *op. cit.*, (n. 52), 171–2, 246–7, Cy. 3.

57 E. Gjerstad, *Opuscula Archaeologica*, 4, 1946, 2–3, pl. 1.

that the moulds of Xeropolis hint at the presence of a Cypriot bronzesmith, turning out tripod legs of ambitious design. And from more recently excavated graves in the royal Toumba cemetery, sophisticated trinkets in gold announce the arrival of another kind of eastern specialist. Already, around 900, we now know of granulated ornaments at Lefkandi,[58] consisting of crescent plates decorated with neat triangles of tiny granules, in a difficult technique forgotten in the Aegean since the demise of the Mycenaean palaces. Nearly 30 years ago, Reynold Higgins[59] reasonably argued that this skill could not have been recovered without tuition from an eastern goldsmith. When he made his case, the earliest granulated work, before the first publication of the Lefkandi cemeteries, was from Athens: the pair of massive plate earrings from the grave of the Rich Lady of the Areopagus,[60] adorned with elaborate designs in granulation and filigree, datable from a fine collection of Attic pottery to around 850 B.C. Soon after, and from a slightly earlier context, came the discovery at Lefkandi of a more daring use of granulation in the round, in the 'mulberry' earrings from Toumba Grave 5.[61] The large and clumsy granules, in Higgins' view, betrayed the hand of a local apprentice rather than an eastern master-jeweller.[62] As a likely source of this new expertise, he looked towards the Phoenician homeland; indeed, one recalls the consummate Phoenician craftsman, remembered in the Homeric poems as a figure familiar to the Greeks, as though he were living among them.[63] And yet, at the risk of claiming too much for Cyprus, I believe that there is a case for looking towards that island for our putative teacher of granulation — or, at least, for the creator of this particular design of earring. The case involves a brief excursion into Homeric archaeology — and here I speak with some trepidation in the original home of that many-sided subject. In these earrings we have by far the closest visual equivalent of the frequently discussed *hermata triglena moroenta*[64] worn by Hera in the Iliad, and by Penelope in the Odyssey: 'earrings with three eyeballs, like mulberries'. But eyeballs do not look like mulberries; here, then, we have to face a puzzle of epic stratification, a puzzle for which a recent find from Cyprus offers one possible solution. To the lowest epic stratum belongs the *moroenta* epithet; for earrings with *single* granulated mulberries, though ultimately of Levantine origin, do indeed occur in the Late

58 In Toumba Grave 59 (LPG-SPG I); M. R. Popham *et al.*, *Archaeological Reports*, 35, 1989, 120, 128, fig. 25; *idem*, in *The Archaeology of Greek Colonisation*, eds. G. R. Tsetskhladze and F. De Angelis, Oxford, 1994, 25, fig. 2.11b; *Lefkandi*, III, pls. 66 (59.26), 136b.

59 R. A. Higgins, *Annual of the British School at Athens*, 64, 1969, 145.

60 E. L. Smithson, *Hesperia*, 37, 1968, 83, 113–14 (no. 77), pl. 32.

61 *Lefkandi*, I, 171 (T. 5.10–11), pls. 171, 231d.

62 R. A. Higgins in *Lefkandi*, I, 221; *idem*, *Greek and Roman Jewellery*, 2nd ed., London, 1980, 106, pl. 16c.

63 C. J. Ruijgh, *L'élément achéen dans la langue épique*, Assen, 1957, 136, remarks on the Phoenician affinities of the name Ikmalios, creator of Penelope's throne in *Odyssey*, xix.55–8. As described by Homer, its resemblance to an ivory throne from Nimrud is remarkable; *cf.* M. E. L. Mallowan, *Illustrated London News*, 1960, 1134–5, figs. 2–4.

64 *Iliad*, xiv.173 (Hera); *Odyssey*, xviii.297–8 (Penelope). Higgins noted the resemblance in *Lefkandi*, I, 221, n. 42.

Bronze Age both of Cyprus and of the Aegean.[65] In Greece, such earrings vanish from the repertoire at the onset of the 'Dark Age'; but in Cyprus they were still being made in a simplified form in the Early Iron Age, as found especially in the tombs of Lapithos.[66] Then, from the ninth century onwards the *triglena* type, an Assyrian invention, came into fashion and also enters the epic repertoire. It is worn by people of high rank in Assyrian reliefs;[67] and, in Cyprus, we have an unusually realistic rendering of three eyeballs from a rich tomb at Amathus, no. 321,[68] in use from the ninth century onwards. Cyprus, then, is the only place which contains all the elements both of the Toumba mulberry earrings and of the somewhat confused Homeric description. Following the island's long tradition of blending ideas from different sources, a Cypriot master-jeweller is a most likely person to hit on the notion of trebling the granulated mulberries in conformity with the three eyeball appendages of the new Assyrian type.

One must, however, observe a sense of proportion in estimating the Cypriot contribution. Cypriot imports, both antique and contemporary, Cypriot iconography, and instruction from skilled Cypriot metalworkers should not blind us to evidence that, as early as the tenth century, the people of Lefkandi were already establishing direct links with the élite of the Phoenician homeland — even if their ships availed themselves of Cypriot ports on their way.[69] In addition to the export of Euboean pottery to Tyre already mentioned, we should also consider the luxurious articles travelling in the reverse direction — especially the splendid set of six faience vases from Toumba Grave 39,[70] the like of which has never been found in any of the numerous tombs excavated in Cyprus; a ring vase, two vessels shaped like bunches of grapes, a lugged amphoriskos, a duck vase, and a plaque in the form of a recumbent feline. Such an extraordinary collection, in a single grave, invites an explanation other than casual trade — as does the genuinely Egyptian faience ring from the same grave, surely a personal possession, with a bust of Amun as a ram's head.[71] The vases, by contrast, are thought to be Egyptianizing work from the Levant rather than true Egyptian;[72] but, in sheer quality, they are none the worse for that. Bearing in mind the distinguished contexts in which similar

65 R. A. Higgins, *Greek and Roman Jewellery*, (n. 62), 86, pl. 12. F. Myres (*Annual of the British School at Athens*, 45, 1950, 237) had already linked them to the *moroenta* earrings.

66 E.g. E. Gjerstad *et al.*, *The Swedish Cyprus Expedition*, vol. I, Stockholm, 1934, pls. 145.8–9, 11, from Lapithos.

67 E.g. R. D. Barnett, *Assyrian Palace Reliefs*, Batchwork Press, London, pl. 16; see also C. Kardara, *American Journal of Archaeology*, 65, 1961, 62–4, pl. 35.

68 *Bulletin de Correspondance Hellénique*, 105, 1981, 1020, fig. 126.

69 For three Euboean LPG vessels from a tomb at Amathus see *op. cit.*, (n. 12), 22, n. 10, pls. 10, 17 (Lim. 46.3–4) with references.

70 *Annual of the British School at Athens*, 77, 1982, 220, T. 39.38–43, pls. 31–2; *Lefkandi*, III, pl. 43.

71 *Annual of the British School at Athens*, 77, 1982, 219–20, 244, fig. 3, pls. 32a–b; *Lefkandi*, III, pl. 43.37.

72 E. J. Peltenburg in *Annual of the British School at Athens*, 77, 1982, 243–5.

vessels occur in the Near East,[73] I should like to air the possibility that this magnificent set came to Lefkandi through a personal link — perhaps even through inter-marriage — between the family of the prince buried in the Toumba building, and a leading family of Tyre.[74]

The foundation of the Tyrian colony at Kition must have lent a new impetus to communications between Cyprus and the Aegean. For that event, much of the dating evidence still awaits full publication; but we know already of a few imports, both Phoenician and Greek,[75] which should put the arrival of the Phoenicians well back in the ninth century. They come from the *Kathari* locality, from the monumental sanctuary of Astarte founded upon the ruins of an indigenous temple site deserted after the eleventh century.[76] But the refurbishment of a derelict ancient sanctuary may not have been the highest priority for the newly arrived colonists, and there may well prove to be some earlier occupation on the *Bamboula* acropolis; there, a much simpler Phoenician shrine has recently come to light, already established in the ninth century, in which Astarte may have been worshipped beside Melqart, Lord of the City.[77] At all events, the coming of the Phoenicians roughly coincides in time with two other developments. First, a massive production in Cyprus of a new ware, Black-on-Red, initially for small unguent flasks, and then adapted for other shapes; a ware copiously represented in a deposit to consecrate the rebuilding of the *Kathari* temple of Astarte after a fire.[78] Second, the trading of these Black-on-Red flasks to Crete and the Dodecanese, the first East Mediterranean fabric to be exported to the Aegean in any quantity. In the North Cemetery of Knossos, for example, the imported Black-on-Red vessels constitute about one percent of the total — quite an impressive proportion in a place always extraordinarily prolific of its own local wares. There, quite soon, the Cypriot imports gave rise to close imitations, as though to advertise the products of a local factory set up under Cypro-Phoenician enterprise, answering a demand for the same delectable contents that filled the original imports.[79] Similar branch factories were set up in the Dodecanese, at first in Cos, and then in Rhodes where, in the eighth century, imports of Black-on-Red were succeeded by Red Slip and, evidently, Cypriot White Painted IV flasks whose Rhodian imitations are seen in the *Kreis und Wellenband*

73 *Ibid.*, 244.

74 I discuss this possibility more fully in another article, 'The first exchanges between Euboeans and Phoenicians: who took the initiative?' in *Mediterranean Peoples in Transition: 13th to early 10th centuries B.C.*, eds., S. Gitin, A. Mazar and E. Stern, Jerusalem, 1998, 353–9.

75 *Kition*, IV, 24–8, 34–5. nos. 24, 36–60, 75, Phoenician; 17–20, nos. 1–4, Greek.

76 V. Karageorghis, *Kition, Mycenaean and Phoenician Discoveries in Cyprus*, London, 1976, 96–7.

77 M. Yon in *Archaeology in Cyprus 1960-1985*, ed. V. Karageorghis, Nicosia, 1985, 223–5, pl. 19.3. P. M. Bikai considers that some of the Phoenician pottery from Kition-*Bamboula* may be as early as the tenth century B.C.; *Biblical Archaeologist*, 1989, 207.

78 V. Karageorghis, *op. cit.*, (n. 76), 108, colour pl. 18.

79 J. N. Coldstream, *Report of the Department of Antiquities, Cyprus*, 1984, 136–7.

aryballoi bearing ornament resembling strands of spaghetti.[80] These elegant little vessels had a wide circulation towards the West, especially in the earliest Greek colony of Pithekoussai,[81] until their popularity was overtaken by a fashion for the more decorative unguent aryballoi of Corinth.

To ascribe this unguent trade to the *Phoenicians* of Cyprus rests partly on the assumption that Black-on-Red ware has a Phoenician origin — an assumption open to criticism from two angles. First, as it appears in Cyprus, Black-on-Red is quite scarce in the mother-city of Tyre and its surroundings, where its occurrences are treated as Cypriot imports.[82] Further south, however, claims have been made for its evolution from a 'Proto-Black-on-Red' phase of flasks made in a heavier, burnished fabric, and found especially in the tombs of Akhziv[83] — the ancient Ecdippa — in the bay of Haifa, near the southern limit of the Phoenician orbit; even so, the question of the ware's origin must remain open until the cemeteries of this important site are fully published. The second objection comes from a recent programme of analysis in the Fitch Laboratory of the British School at Athens,[84] which found that Black-on-Red pottery, as we know it in Cyprus, is an exclusively Cypriot product, exported to both ends of the Levant, to Al Mina in the north and to Tels Ajjul and Fara in the extreme south; no samples, however, were taken from the central Levant. This conclusion does not surprise me, and perhaps the genesis of Black-on-Red can be explained as an earlier instance of what happened later in the eastern unguent factories set up in Cos, Rhodes and Crete; that is, Phoenician merchants bottling unguents in fine-walled containers made by skilled local artisans, both for local use and for export further afield. If these containers owed anything to an earlier and heavier Phoenician ware, this would not be the first time that the expert potters of Cyprus took over, and vastly improved upon, a foreign idea.[85] Through the enterprise of Cypro-Phoenician traders, their products were exported to, and imitated in the Aegean; thus, long before the widespread circulation of Protocorinthian aryballoi, the amenity of choice unguents, bottled in small and delicate containers, was reintroduced to Greece from Cyprus.

---

80 J. N. Coldstream, *Bulletin of the Institute of Classical Studies (London)*, 18, 1969, 1–8, pls. 1–2.

81 D. Ridgway, *The First Western Greeks*, Cambridge, 1992, 60–62, fig. 13.5; G. Buchner and D. Ridgway, *Pithekoussai*, I, 733, Aryballos (x), 'importato' K(reis und) W(ellenband) originale', nearly one hundred examples listed.

82 P. M. Bikai, *The Pottery of Tyre*, Warminster, 1978, 53, 'Import 1'; S. Chapman, *Berytus*, 21, 1972, 178, notes the rarity of Black-on-Red in the region of Tyre (e.g. 144–5, fig. 31) but leaves open the possibility of an origin in 'some localized part' of Phoenicia.

83 M. W. Prausnitz, 'Red-Polished and Black-on-Red Wares at Akhziv . . .' in *Proceedings of the 1st International Cyprological Congress*, April 1969, eds. V. Karageorghis and A. Christodoulou, Nicosia, 1972, 151–6; *ibid*, in *Phönizier im Westen*, ed. H.–G. Niemeyer, *Madrider Beiträge*, 8, Mainz, 1982, 38–9; *cf*. W. Culican in *op. cit.*, 55–61.

84 N. J. Brodie and L. Steel, 'Cypriot Black-on-Red Ware: towards a characterisation', *Archaeometry*, 38.2, 1996, 263–78.

85 I examine this possibility more fully in a forthcoming paper, 'Crete and the Dodecanese: alternative eastern approaches to the Greek world during the Geometric period', in *International Symposium: Eastern Mediterranean: Cyprus, Dodecanese, Crete, 1500–500 B.C.*, Rethymnon, 13–16 May, 1997.

In conclusion, to define the Cypriot contribution more sharply, we should bear in mind what did *not* come to Greece from Cyprus. Literacy, forgotten in Greece for over three centuries, had never wholly died out in Cyprus. From Tomb 49 at Palaepaphos-*Skales* we have the inscription of a Greek proper name, Opheltas, on a bronze spit, showing that the syllabic script of the Late Cypriot Bronze Age had already been adapted for writing Greek no later than the early tenth century;[86] but, if early Euboean visitors to the island had ever encountered this cumbersome form of writing, they showed no sign of wishing to learn it. Instead, the Aegean Greeks preferred the alphabetic system of the Phoenicians which, as Dr Jeffery demonstrated,[87] must have been acquired in a place where Aegean Greeks and Phoenicians were living in close enough proximity to overcome the language barrier. Could Kition have been such a place? This I doubt, since we have no evidence of Greek traders actually residing there before or during the time of transmission.[88]

Likewise, from the ninth century onwards, early Greek visitors to Kition must have seen and admired the splendid ashlar architecture of the Astarte temple; but, in Greece, the earliest moves towards monumental building are not seen until the seventh century,[89] perhaps in response to a demand for fine urban temples to cement the *esprit de corps* of the emergent *polis*. In the Greek kingdoms of Cyprus, the entirely different nature of worship was memorably outlined by Myres himself in his catalogue of the Cesnola collection.[90] Their sanctuaries, unlike those in Greece, required no impressive monumental temples; all that was needed was a sacred enclosure, an altar as the focus of worship, and a small recess for the storing of sacred furniture and surplus offerings. In the open air, crowded around the altar, were hordes of votive terracotta statues representing the worshippers and interceding for them, clothed according to the current fashion, and made in various sizes according to the means and status of the votaries; the most memorable illustration comes from Gjerstad's excavation of the rustic sanctuary at Ayia Irini.[91] As Myres put it,[92] '. . . religious acts took time, which the votary could ill spare from the daily round; . . . To maintain continuous communion, while "man goeth forth to

86 V. Karageorghis, *Palaepaphos-Skales*, pls. T. 49.15, 61, fig. 89.

87 L. H. Jeffery, *The Local Scripts of Archaic Greece*, 2nd edn., Oxford, 1990, 1–2.

88 The lack of interest in the Greek-Cypriot syllabary weighs against the theory advanced by A. Heubeck in *Archaeologica Homerica, X: Schrift*, Göttingen, 1979, 85–7, that literate Cyprus could have acted as a catalyst towards the acquisition of literacy by the Aegean Greeks. This hypothesis is discussed by A. W. Johnston in *The Greek Renaissance of the 8th Century B.C.*, ed. R. Hägg, Stockholm, 1983, 66–7. Very recently, the Cypriot hypothesis has been revived by R. D. Woodard, *Greek Writing from Knossos to Homer*, California, 1997.

89 J. J. Coulton, *Greek Architects at Work*, London, 1977, ch. 2.

90 J. L. Myres, *op. cit.*, (n. 5), 123–9.

91 E. Gjerstad *et al.*, *The Swedish Cyprus Expedition*, vol. II, Stockholm, 1935, 642–824, esp. 799, fig. 277; vol. IV.2, 3–4.

92 *Loc. cit.*, (n. 90), 127.

his work and to his labour", continuous attendance was essential; but primitive thought permitted the substitution of an effigy'. To return, then, to the matter mentioned at the beginning of this paper: in the middle of the seventh century, life-sized sculpture emerged in Greece and in Cyprus at about the same time but, as Myres saw, on quite independent lines: in Cyprus, vast terracotta figures of worshippers made in sections on the wheel and fitted together;[93] in Greece, statues of deities, or of aristocrats beside their tombs, based on a flat, almost two-dimensional style of Levantine terracottas, enlarged to life size in Cycladic marble or Cretan limestone.[94] A little later,, both in Cyprus and in Greece, instruction in working stone for truly three-dimensional figures came in different ways from Egypt, the only land with an unbroken tradition in that form of art. But we have already travelled some way beyond any age that can possibly be called 'Dark'.

Wherein, then, lies the Cypriot contribution towards the lightening of the Greek 'Dark Age'? Not so much in artistic influence, except — initially — through antiques of the Cypriot Late Bronze Age, circulating at large in the Aegean, and stimulating the imagination of Greek craftsmen during the early part of their 'Dark Age'. Later, with the revival of commerce, the Black-on-Red unguent trade in the Aegean seems like the work of Cypro-Phoenician entrepreneurs newly established in their colony of Kition. Otherwise, what Cyprus offered was, above all, lessons in the working of metal: in ironworking, especially in the difficult technique of carburization; probably in the fashioning of bronze tripod cauldrons, both in enlivening their decoration and in increasing their size to become objects of prestige; possibly in granulated goldwork, combining traditional Bronze-Age forms with new oriental notions in a typically Cypriot way. It is easy to see how all these techniques could have been transmitted from Cypriot Greeks to Aegean Greeks, across a minimal language barrier that cannot ever have been totally insurmountable.

93 E. Gjerstad, *The Swedish Cyprus Expedition*, vol. IV.2, Stockholm, 1948, 94–7.

94 R. M. Cook, *Journal of Hellenic Studies*, 87, 1967, 24–32.

J. L. MYRES MEMORIAL LECTURES